From Opal
Xmas 1974

OREGON

POETS:

ARTISTS:
Robert Huck
Nelson Sandgren

OREGON
STATE
COLLEGE
1959

EDITORS:
R. D. Brown
Thomas Kranidas
Faith G. Norris

Signatures

ACKNOWLEDGMENTS

ANGUS & ROBERTSON for "Winter Ploughing," "Kookaburras," "Bottle Swallows," "Red Charlie," "Thrift," and "After the Fire" from *Cut from Mulga;* for "Hold Dear Things Not Too Close" from *Brief Waters;* for "Spider" from *The Lifted Spear;* and for "Wife to Second Husband" from *Beware the Cuckoo.* ATLANTIC for "Colonel Johnson's Ride," "King Salmon," "Catamount," and "Child on a Pullman." BOTTEGHE OSCURE for "The Hare," "The Long Corners," "Entrance Into the City," "For the Grave of Daniel Boone," and "Thirteen Great Ladies." COLLEGE ENGLISH for "Heart of the Matter." COLORADO QUARTERLY for "The Old Scout," "Doubt on the Great Divide," "Bicycle," "Homecoming" here renamed "Appearances" and "In the Tide Ponds." FOLIO for "Rainbow." KANSAS MAGAZINE for "Cold Country Ballad." THE NATION for "Homecoming." NEW CAMPUS WRITING for "Postcards from Scappoose." NEW MEXICO QUARTERLY for "Before the Big Storm." NEW ORLEANS POETRY JOURNAL for "Farewell and Hail." NEW WORLD WRITING for "Summerhouse." THE NEW YORKER for "The Ballad of Red Fox." NORTHWEST REVIEW for "Brahman." PARIS REVIEW for "Blue Fruit," and "Requiem." POETRY for "The Snows," "Things We Did That Meant Something," "In Bailey Woods," "The Hunt Within," "Elk," "Night at the Fish Traps," "The Delay," "A Now Famous Escape," and "Flowering Antler." PRAIRIE SCHOONER for "New Mexico in Retrospect," "Hunters," "Holding the Sky," and "Fall Journey." SATURDAY REVIEW for "Minstrel," "At the Custer Monument." CHARLES SCRIBNER'S SONS for "A Christmas Card." ALAN SWALLOW for "Old Fishstation" and "Ski Song," "Fireweed," "High Desert" from *Several Houses.* TALISMAN for "The Research

INTRODUCTION

Oregon Signatures has grown out of a series of poetry readings sponsored by the Liberal Arts Lectures Committee at Oregon State College. It was a happy accident that Oregon's centennial year coincided with the beginning of this series and has made possible in part the financing of this book.

From the start, the readings have featured the work of Oregon poets who have published in national and international magazines; when we came to choose the contributors to this volume, we kept in mind not only the general public but also the audiences who had desired to see this poetry made more accessible.

Since occasional poetry seldom lives beyond the occasion of its writing, we did not request work inspired by the centennial or the history or the scenery of the state. Instead, we required of the poets only that they submit their best work. Happily for a book designed to publicize one Oregon product, some common and distinctive themes did appear. What these themes are, we leave to the reader to determine, confident that he will find the search rewarding.

The artists did not have so easy a time; although the subject matter of their work was their own choice, budget problems demanded only work that could be reproduced by letterpress. The results have been happy; those who know the prints of Mr. Huck and the water colors of Mr. Sandgren may be disappointed at not finding the color for which both men are justly known but will applaud their accomplishment in difficult circumstances.

A striking example of the enthusiasm this project has aroused in our contributors should be mentioned: all the poets and artists agreed that the profits from this work would go to a fund at OSC for the publication of further fine arts books, an example of human and poetic virtue worthy of comment in any century.

On behalf of the poets and artists here represented, the editors wish to thank the Oregon Centennial Commission in the persons of Mr. James S. Hart, Chairman of the Fine Arts Commission, and Mr. Arthur Kreisman, Chairman of the sub-committee for Literary Events, for their generosity and understanding.

We are equally indebted to the Faculty Publications Committee of Oregon State College; their willingness to enter a new field of publication indicates a future of continuing accomplishment in the fine arts at Oregon State College as well as in the state of Oregon.

Finally, to Professor Herbert B. Nelson and the members of the English Department at Oregon State College, we make this acknowledgment of sponsorship that was both immediate and practical.

R. D. BROWN
THOMAS KRANIDAS
FAITH G. NORRIS

Oregon State College
Corvallis, 1959

T. E. LAWRENCE TRANSLATED AS MINOR DEITY

"Close round them lapped the dark wormwood, now heavy
with dew, in which the ends of the moonbeams sparkled like
sea-spray. The corpses seemed flung so pitifully on the
ground, huddled anyhow in low heaps. Surely if straight-
ened they would be comfortable at last. So I put them all
in order, one by one." *Seven Pillars of Wisdom.*

His hope lets down its tendrils through the leaves
In search of life along the acrid air.
He sends himself among the dead, and grieves.
His shadow floods the hills, and everywhere
His feet and hair, his fingertips and nose
From marble into massive coral turn,
For into simple flame he cannot burn.
Instead, he offers up a glowing rose.

How cool and still the pools within their eyes.
At home in England, now the fields are green.
He walks upon the deep, without disguise,
From formal gardens to this burning scene:
The broken wheels, the violated wells,
The dead he lays in rows like cockleshells.

SONG

This our love and motion
To lie among the strings
Where wind divides the wind
And summer above our heads.

Where now the spider builds
In a chorus of old repair
His winter of torn threads
And spreads his arms along,

1

To where our bodies ride
The tangled roots and rings,
The stiff, the dying song
Sung by a broken string.

PASTORELA

(after Marcabru)
Beside a hedge the other day
I found a common shepherdess
Teeming with wit and joyfulness,
The daughter of a common mother.
She wore a cloak and coat of fur,
But underneath I spied her shirt
Of heavy stuff, like woolen drill.

I rode to her across the plain.
Maiden, I said, O charming thing,
I see the cold is stinging you.
Sir, said the common shepherdess,
Because of God and my old nurse
Winds that keep my hair disheveled
Are nothing: I feel strong and gay.

Maiden, I said, O sweetest thing,
I pulled aside from the straight road
To rest and talk with you awhile,
For such a common shepherdess
Should not attend her flocks alone
Without a brave companion near.
The fields are bare and desolate.

Lord, she said, whatever I am
I know a fool is not a wit.
It seems to me your bravery,
Sir, said the common shepherdess,
Should keep the road it took at first,
For many men who think they own
Their peership, only boast of it.

Maiden, maiden of noble birth,
Your father must have been a knight,
Your mother, too, an honored maid
Raised from a common shepherdess.
The more I look, your beauty grows,
And I am happy through your joy;
O be more human just for once.

Lord, she said, my simple birth,
If I go back, and not too far,
Harks to the sickle and the plough,
Sir, said the common shepherdess.
But many men turn into knights
Who should, as their forefathers did,
Work every day from dawn to dark.

Maiden, I said, the lovely witch
That gave to you a noble birth,
And grace abounding from the earth
Beyond a common shepherdess,
Would not object to watch it grow
Beyond the bounds of kin and kind
If you lay underneath me there.

Lord, is it too much to ask
A little less reward from you?
You raise me high in praise today,
Sir, said the common shepherdess,
Tomorrow, when the wind is worse,
I know what I would get from you:
Chatter enough to think upon.

Maiden, a high and rueful heart
Is often claimed by careful art.
As I was riding here to you
I thought: that common shepherdess
Might consent to tumble with me
Upon this hill in jollity.
If we could only hold our tongues.

Lord, a man set on by folly
Swears and pledges and promises
As you have courted me today,
Sir, said the common shepherdess.
But this is not a fair exchange:
My maidenhood, for your high praise,
To find that I am called a slut.

Maiden, look, how every creature
Must return to its own nature.
O should we not, then meet as mates
But once, my lonely shepherdess,
Inside your hut upon the hill;
The wind cannot get at you there,
I know a game to keep you warm.

Lord, recall what reason says:
The fool is searching for his folly,
As the knight searches for his lady,
Swains, for a common shepherdess.
For surely he has lost his mind
Who can't follow the road he starts:
And this too, is a gilded 'saw.'

Maiden, hear me, I've never seen
From far a more deceptive face,
Or looked closer on a falser heart.
Sir, you're under a fearful spell,
For you do not know how to tell
The image from the living art,
A wooden from a silver bell.

BLUE FRUIT

Now the blue fruit
And frosty weeds decay;
Now, October's root
Weaves below the shade.

Old and golden pears
Hang still upon the stem;
Smell up the county air
And all my county kin;

Who stacked and pitched in fields
The stick, the golden grain,
Around the polished hills
Tore down the summer's rain.

Now the cold stones
Crack below the wall;
Send the crooked hare
A crooked mile or more;

Where every eye pegs
That rabbit toward his keep;
But, startled by a keg
Of apples in their sleep,

Weaves against the sun
Under the tilted ground,
Where great kilns burn
The hills without a sound.

THE SLEEPER

This is a castle and a burning grove.
This is a man who was deeply in love.

This, the same who, wandering, came
Into the heart of the spinning flame,

Stormed the gates, and thru the grove
Wove into her whom he could not move;

Crying aloud, oh the world must hear,
How, in the night, with trembling fear,

Out of the sleeping part of his love,
She came to him in the burning grove.

THE DEATH OF THE MILLER

I

Inside, the walls are clad with moss and clay,
As smooth, as rough as curds and whey.
The massive axle, tapering to still stone,
Turns quiet now like his shank bone.

The water drops, so slow, so slow, it seems
To fall, like dew, among the beams.
His gliding swans, adrift across the race,
Immaculate, recall his grace.

II

We towed him seaward, rowing with the tide
Retreating down the river's side.
Falling, alluvial, over the shallow shoals,
The water stood above the holes,
Where, like weeds, into the current's light,
His fish came cunningly to sight.
We placed his body in his open boat,
And used for sails his dusty coat.

III

Outside, the wooden pads are turned and wheeled
And walk his river like a field
Of standing grain; the mowers, singing, scythe
From gold to common ore for tythe.

They load the sheaves on wagons at their wills,
But jog behind them down the hills.
There, beside the race, they watch the sun,
On nimble stilts, begin its run.

IV

From dusk to dawn, inside the mill, all night
His women work beside the light.
They shear the cords that bind each golden head,
And sighing, make a second bed
Of sound from which his spirit, naked, shags
In waves of song above the hags:
Who barricade the door, the gate, the wheel
Against the deadly, flying meal.

SONNET NUMBER TWO

My second sonnet rises like a clear day.
The first, beyond my reach; its pale sestet
Awash with local tones; its cold octet
A shallow sullen thing; the whole, decay.

I hug the water, clamour shoreward, wet.
A grove of trees ahead; their dark, a piece;
The moon, a jot, but brackish with increase;
The sounds of night draw near; their tone is set.

And so, impatient, I await the light.
And walk, and shift the atmosphere, and read,
And drive Marvèll from page to page, and write,
And ask, if art (his nature) warms the dead?

Impulsive, wretched, weary as rankled skin,
I feel the dawn come back, the dark within.

THE HARE

The snows in single treason mock the earth;
Or nearly mock, with birth of fallen barrows,
As winter spins her light alloys for death.
At steep and tangled undergrowth, at furrows,
The shallow sun returns with baited breath.

Under the boughs, there, in shrouds of sound,
On a high hill, the milk-white hare, awakes,
Withdraws beyond this once-protective ground;
As wind in stylus motion works the flakes,
To hide his movement from the silvered hound.

THE LONG CORNERS

The long, stiff fingers of his father's hand
Rose and fell, fell and beat, like bands
Of straight and narrow sticks on his smooth skin.
He stood quiet and still, holding—

Light dropped toward him.
Boards rolled out of a high window.
Up the bright and crested stairs
And down the darkened hall he ran
Into the room, square and cold.
He stood deep in the center,
Staring down into the long corners.
The hard floor tilted.
The table ran into the window.
A door swung free. Nails fell
Loud to the floor. Light lowered,
As the ceiling slammed down the walls.

Silently then he slipped
Beneath the bed's springs,
And heard, for the first time,
The coiled wires rub on his bare back.

Robert Huff

RAINBOW

After the shot the driven feathers rock
In the air and are by sunlight trapped.
Their moment of descent is eloquent.
It is the rainbow echo of a bird
Whose thunder, stopped, puts in my daughter's eyes
A question mark. She does not see the rainbow,
And the folding bird-fall was for her too quick.
It is about the stillness of the bird
Her eyes are asking. She is three years old;
Has cut her fingers; found blood tastes of salt;
But she has never witnessed quiet blood,
Nor ever seen before the peace of death.
I say: "The feathers—Look!" but she is torn
And wretched and draws back. And I am glad
That I have wounded her, have winged her heart,
And that she goes beyond my fathering.

FIREFIGHTER

When I see lightning I remember red:
Squirrels running before the fuel red;
Crisp noises heard by moles in mole runs red
With roots like rivets; windmade, bouncing red
Balls in the tops of trees; bats burning; red
Moonlight; the timber all night flashing, red
At dawn, black stalks at noon; the barren, red,
Hot-ash waste with the last sparks going dead.

I don't want lightning now or when I'm dead.
The downed men weep for light and get the dead,
White, cold kind, and the fires, too. Their dead
Hearts burn; their shadows shake before the dead
Glow when the King of Flame kindles the dead
Stumps with his lightning bolts. Those tails are dead
Set to be powerful; making that dead
World hot, they flash, making this live world red.

KING SALMON

A gravel deathbed for the king of fish.
Nuncle, the mad Kingfisher had you hooked
From birthrise, hauled and schooled, and heaved
From saltsea silver up brown rapids run
To rest your milt-white crown upon these stones.
Hear how the windy guts of gulls
Rejoice above your ghost beginning now.
They growl for so much Godspent majesty.

You are alone and home now, nuncle. Rest.
The carcasses of all your rock-whipped sons
Will boil this stream where famished birds
Wheel as their fathers wheeled and rose and fell.
To rest in rotting flesh is sanity.
Die well, for you were most mad all your life,
Left every quaking net torn in your wake,
Ended the painful flight of being born.

HUNTERS

Especially when it's foggy men are fooled
By birds, beasts, and the skeletal remains
Of stumpy trees; when it's frosty by leaves;
And almost any time at all by sound.
So poetry can happen to the mind
If senses want to make the beautiful.

An old man listening in a blind can feel
That every wildfowl he has killed is still
Alive, because his ears are filled, and think
That fog contains within its wary world
His first love with her pack of flying hounds
And let sounds make a bower of his blind.

Young men who look into the mist at dawn
May see the beast unclearly and declare
The image brings a fever on; that deer
Are seen whose antlers cannot fall, whose heads
Shall grace no trophy walls; and that they are
Afraid before a perfect animal.

And there are men who hunt for ghostly trees.
These sawyers have been known to wince and cry,
Her pain, the old hag's, hear her falling pain.
As if they found old snags unnatural
Or men became their natures' best when fooled,
Their voices made their actions beautiful.

BRAHMAN

> "It does not seem much, still
> it is more than I am myself."
> —*A Passage to India.*

The day the white bull sailed out it was lovely
In the crowd. We heard the gate swing open,
Cow bell clang, saw him and rider flying,
Heard the roar. They flew apart before it stopped,
The Brahman landing near a lonesome clown.
We made that noise together out of one mouth,
Fathers, mothers, everyone, because
A white bull might have killed a man,
Or a man might have ridden a white bull,
Or just because together we could sound
Like nothing but humanity, so that
That empty, humpbacked creature came with bell
A-tinkling, stopped, and stared into the stands
As if we were one lovely looking cow.

WITH THOMAS HARDY

What are the mountain flowers doing?
Where are the wings and lucky feet?

Warm and the world have done with wooing.
Nothing that takes to air is sweet.

What of the bees, their hives, the honey,
The golden light they keep within?

You have sold out for meat and money,
Madness, maids and yellow gin.

Only a little sound I'm saying
As if we held together here.

Nothing at all like swarms and swaying,
Nothing you really need to hear.

THE SNOWS

As sudden as the geese the first snow was,
Patterned and shaping summer: so we fell
Into the absolution of our seeds'
Affluent piety and knew the Sun,
The blessing Sun, burned white eternity.

Still, came the late snow. The barking birds moved on
And soon were gone, leaving a cotton sound
In the air, the muffled steeples looming strong
Above layers of silence: and we fell,
Abandoned, to the ringing of the bells.

CATAMOUNT

Crouched in the center of my sight
The cougar treed at Crawford Springs
Still whips his dogged tail down and waits for me.
Light moves like leaves along his side,
His eyes among the shadows hide,
The beast controls the swinging of his tail.

I dragged the hounds home years ago,
Thinking myself most righteous then,
But I was running nearly all the way,
That Hades-heavy half of man
Astride me all the time I ran,
Lashing the air behind me with his tail.

COLONEL JOHNSON'S RIDE

This morning, rolling through a cloud
Around a mountain on clear ice,
He listens to small hail beat down. The loud
Tick of it sounds almost like rice

Tossed at the windshield. . . . There was a bride
Beside him once, an isolated heart,
Something like water snuggled at his side,
But he's had rotten fishing from the start.

And she's behind him, landlocked in their bed.
Wrapped in her own groundcloud of winter dreams,
How does she move? Whom does she wed
While sea-run rainbows, separate, fight the streams

Below and he goes circling down,
Precariously skidding till he stops
Outside the fog drift, sees dawn crown
Like fire on the mountain tops,

And gets out, touchy, near the river bank?
For beauty, ever since his wedding night
He's known he has his own hard self to thank.
He's come alone to sound this water right.

THE SMOKER

Sitting down near him in the shade,
I watch him strike a match on his white cane.
He burns his finger but displays no pain.
This smiling blind man with a hearing aid

Smokes by the hour. Now he's blowing rings.
He measures in the smoke and takes much care
To shape his mouth for pumping circled air.
He fathers hundreds of round hoverings.

16

I offer: It's too warm; it ought to rain.
His only comment is a smiling cough.
Maybe he's got his hearing aid turned off
To keep such interference from his brain,

Or can't hear through the haze, or won't let sound
Disturb his gentle passion. Who can tell
What he envisions with his sense of smell
Heaving my presence at him by the pound?

I never blame him when he comes in dreams,
A slow smile smoking, circled to the thighs,
And screws both of his thumbs into my eyes
And will not stop to listen to my screams.

SECOND BURNING

Just a little bit like that man in Wisconsin
Who dressed out the middle-aged carcass
Of a barmaid and probably floated back
To his parlor to rock amid dry head bones,
Ribs, thighs and the finally immaculate pelvis,

When I was sure our old bitch was gone in the eyes—
Cataracts, sties—two sea stones with their juice
Eating her nose, I brought a new-filed axe down quick
And made a clean division; carried her by the ear
In one hand, hind leg in the other, to a pyre

Behind the barn, and oiled and burned her.
But rites on farms are habits like small killing.
I'm lucky in my dreams when I can climb the high loft
On a shaky ladder, spit at that axe, and tremble,
Giddy as a green-cheeked boy poking a breathless pigeon.

THE CURE

First, death of exultation in Toledo
Left me afraid of touching even flowers,
Then settled on the soft part of my ego
As towels do on bottles after hours.

Returning home, I kept my small discovery
Behind the shades and would have stayed within,
But family prayers voiced for my quick recovery
Needled me into town to drink again.

My clammy ghost went with me, paleness pending,
And would have hovered so, had I been lazy
And not drunk into shapes all that is ending
And beat them up until my fists went crazy.

MINSTREL

All envious of fish and fowl,
Good beasts, and then sweet ladies, I began.

But trout once torn from water cried,
"You haven't got the hook inside."
And resurrected pheasants flew my bag.

The ladies I was singing for
Walked through the room and out the door.
My notes went lonesome from the hunting horn.

Being thus envious of bait,
I placed three worms upon a plate;
I danced around them till the floor got warm.

They made a perfect audience,
And I've attempted nothing since
Save digging worms to dance for when I can.

18

Melvin Walker La Follette

THIRTEEN GREAT LADIES

Thirteen great ladies, arrayed in green,
Walked beside a grey stone wall;
Thirteen greyhounds, lank and lean,

Attended our ladies, and walked between
Our ladies and the grey stone wall.
Thirteen great ladies, arrayed in green.

Mincing through meadows, they were seen
Cutting green willow whistles to call
Thirteen greyhounds, lank and lean.

With eyes of thirsty fire, hot and mean,
A dragon paced within his grey stone stall.
Thirteen great ladies, arrayed in green,

Failed to see this baneful scene
Because there walked, between them and the wall,
Thirteen greyhounds, lank and lean.
Alas! The dragon, hot and mean,
Leapt through the wall, devouring all
Thirteen great ladies, arrayed in green,
Thirteen greyhounds, lank and lean.

THE BALLAD OF RED FOX

Yellow sun yellow
Sun yellow sun,
When, oh, when
Will red fox run?

When the hollow horn shall sound,
When the hunter lifts his gun
And liberates the wicked hound
Then, oh, then shall red fox run.

21

Yellow sun yellow
Sun yellow sun,
Where, oh, where
Will red fox run?

Through meadows hot as sulphur,
Through forests cool as clay,
Through hedges crisp as morning
And grasses limp as day.

Yellow sky yellow
Sky yellow sky,
How, oh, how
Will red fox die?

With a bullet in his belly,
A dagger in his eye,
And blood upon his red red brush
Shall red fox die.

SAINT MARTIN AND THE BEGGAR

(After a painting by El Greco)

I

Some say he sought for models in the mad,
Finding in chains, the stare within the stare;
Lifting the manacled youth, the babbling lad
To cleaner heights upon his snowy mare;
Saved from cage's filth, the lad might wear
A crown of golden thorns, or be amused
To run his hand across his snake-filled hair,
Or caught out in light, to find his back abused
By whips no more, but clothed as it was used,
So long ago, in cloaks, by mother hands
Drawn fine and velvet; even to be confused

22

With what most holy is: he understands
The nature of darkness and the saints'
Long night, as furious in the rhythmic dark, he paints.

II
Some petaled lad, with arms as white as girls,
Leading him through the granite groin of dark,
Might whisper as the splendour of his curls
Surprises light; the bridle cuts an arc
Of flaming green upon the snowy neck,
And tangles with the green that stings his eyes,
And purples on his breast a secret mark;
Spelled in his shadowed walk, the white mare shies
Not from him, whose kindly hands are wise
Beyond greed, remembering still the chain
That bound them to the deep: the painter cries
Alone, the sinful witness to God's pain
Run wild; fore-agonized, but not fore-
Warned, the wound of God wakes screaming from his sore.

SUMMERHOUSE

There have been three storms in my heart
Since the apricot blossomed; the gourd
Where the purple martens nested is empty;
Oh, goodbye. There is one room that I
Must not touch. It is furnished with a hoard
Of treasures. I recall, with a start,
There was something in June I forgot,
When the storm clouds fumed, lazy and hot,
Over the orchard. In July, I could fling
Dry clods at the noisy birds. Something
Spoke. That was the second storm. In August
A whirlwind filled my mouth with dust,
And I cried. It is September; the lost
Room is locked, my heart is attuned to frost

ON THE DEATHS OF BIRDS
LA MORT NY MORD

I

A man is watching, where the sapphire jay
Is crested in fir boughs, blueing and greening the sunlight;
A beautiful boy is walking through the meadow,
By a fresh spring he stoops, and gargling the water
Spits over stones, where incipient trout lurk;

The boy is alarmed, and turns his head with a jerk
When the man moves toward him, making a killdeer scatter
Into the brush with her gangling chick, but, Oh!
There is joy in the boy's fear, a night
Of knowledge within the body of his day.

The secret of power is birds, their element
Is water, sky, and earth, and everywhere
They fly like souls, and they are innocent
Of everything but grace and light and color.

II

The boy smiles, the man sings, and from his high
Height a bird whistles into the happy sky,
Whose wings are red. And many birds in the wood
Whose heads beaks breasts and backs are red
Are whistling too. The boy laughs, he
Sees the light bleed rainbows, though the thud
Scares the birds.
                    The boy screams, and every
Red vermillion scarlet madder blood
And flame hued bird that ever pipped a shell is killed;
The boy's smile is frozen; his scream is stilled.

24

And we are trapped among the songless dead
Whose beauty flutters in the ebbing flood.
You clutch my hand and mutter, outraged by this out-
    rageous thing,
But I smile now, hearing the music: not one, but two men
    sing.

THE SONG

The boy is walking into the wood alone,
Armed with the kisses his mother gave him; now,
Just as darkness swallows the brightest glade,
He finds a hut the way he knew he would.

It is not a witch, but a siren who opens the door,
Very voluptuous, who could ask for more?
But the boy loves his mother; at least, he thinks he should,
And bids the siren farewell;

                  the shadows fade
Into a pond of moonlight; his face, the prow
Of Argo sweeping toward the whirling stone.
Why does the siren gnash her teeth and groan?
No wax stops his ears, no fever sends him on;

The boy stands up and sings the siren's tune
Under the sad, manipulated moon.

FROM *SONGS OF ARION:*
II

I DO NOT HEAR YOU CRY, ALTHOUGH THE WOUND
Fell deep, and choked at you, and caught your blood
No. You do not weep. Your eyes, your head,
Your body grows and trembles with a sound
Like music, and a fragrance builds around
Your quiet face like roses, though a thistle
Pricks your side instead, and a bob-white's whistle
Lingers to cheer your bed upon the ground.

It was not always thus. I have seen your tears
Reflect like mirrors through the falling years:
I climbed the higher tree, but when you tried
To follow me, you fell among the roses;
I clowned to make you laugh, still laughing when you cried:
"Being a child, I cry when I am hurt."

V

WHEN WE HAD TRACKED THE COUGAR TO HER LAIR,
Tracing the spoor of blood through the crusted snow,
And after I had found her crumpled there
In the entrance, I cried. I cried and did not know
That you were watching me from the ledge below;
I did not know death was such a surprise
Till you tugged at my sleeve and asked me "please, let's go"
As I lifted her head with my hands and closed her eyes.

Now you importune me, saying you are wise
To the ways of the hunt, the sickness of the kill,
And now you come begging me that I advise
You in new ways of chace, who are the victor still;
Should I, whose tears were all the mother knew,
Instruct you how to kill the litter, too?

VI

IF THERE IS LOVE BETWEEN US, LET IT FEED
On single sorrows to compound its growth
Until it bears upon its limbs, like seed,
A double harvest that confounds us both;
Your moonlit face excites my heart to barter
Bright things for dark, the tame things for the wild;
I stand before you quick as any child
To strike a trade with you for all your treasure.

Let us exchange: my red-gold columbines,
My earliest dogtooth violet that forces
Its head through the snow, the tawny sun that shines
Upon my house, my yellow cat; your pines,
Your meadow interspersed with watercourses,
Your owls, your desert, and your wild horses.

IX

NOR HERO AM I NOW, NOR KING, NOR NO
Wight worthy of your notice or your grace;
Nor wild beast am I, but naked man,
Whose body curves against the surge of space
And hugs the cup of air that holds your song;
Nor is there now a sign that you can know
Me by, no more than any other
Garden wanderer whose tale began
In the long-told sin, the long-slain younger brother.

Still, there is certain proof that I belong
To you, for like a king I give you choice
Of everything I have: my hero's brawn,
My bear's dumb brain, my able skin, my voice
That sings your music, after you have gone.

XI

SEEING YOUR FACE AGAIN, I AM REMINDED
How little I loved you when you were away;
The early air has cracked by defective clay,
Too frail from your fire; this hazel wand has bended
Toward water sweet and holier than yours;
But do not abuse my fickleness with tears,
For I respect the god you have befriended;
My journey through the life of you has ended.

Still, it is with true pain that I relinquish
The chart that held me in your element;
If prayers could be heard, I would have one wish
Come true, and that one innocent:
I wish I could forget the day we kissed
Beneath the tallest cedar in the forest.

Frederick Starr

THIS MEREST SPRING

Rain seems less kind than it was formerly;
legs stiffen forcing upwind.
The circle of the weather is worn.

And I imagine now
that winter is no worse than summer,
less so both than spring.

For the springtime enters
with loss of the first nakedness and the last.

Walking here in April,
unresurrected among the colors,
blind to the successful whiteness
of cherry and pear, time of the body
brings to its past seasons the arrogant mind.
As then so now: alternate withdrawal
and search past the limen into beyond searching;
then recourse to the symbol made of substance
like fog of the year's queer thinness drawn to fine scent
of orchards, here in this merest spring.

Strolling in April there is much to remember
of always becoming never was.

And the eyes
see again at the border of grass and gravel,
stare into vertical stone, witness
the clear waterbraids weaving
under the black winter.

SWITCHYARD

Anesthetize the distance, haul at its skein,
wind it under the treeless scarp of a mind
whose spaces echo the beating of live steam
upon the powerful kettledrum of midnight.

The brain-net swarms with shadow; statuesque
the stasis of the dark while the steam engine
knocks on the drum, drums on the heavy membrane
and starts awareness flickering through moon miles.

An elephantine shuffle, then the pause.
Some brother monster wails from the abyss,
hurling integral godlessness through atoms
in steel harness rocketing far down night.

The drumhead twitches thunder under the nerves
illuminating, as that lumbering beast
who crouched in quiet stalks again the rails
to call an earth beyond our most primitive being

back through the tightly whispering skin of midnight—
posthumous tongues raising a quiet prayer's
unaspirated longing, world without end,
the dream before the dreamer was at hand.

IN REMEMBRANCE OF ROBERT G. LEWIS

(d. May 19, 1949)
Greater than the seabath is its silence
stupendous like the sky, open, admirable,
an element to laze in, a restless solvent
of stone and bone and the pathetic flesh
mouthless with memories.

Sea, do you remember
him, how you took him, your midnight comer
who tumbled through shadows to your uncritical calm,
hissed out his life against you, folded
his fire in your total forever unfolding
forever in your tides?

And how shall the forever
remember, that rolling essence with its salt shine
heedless by archipelagoes?

How shall any
completeness deep with light-unvisited depths
in that cold self-evenness know?

Ocean feels through to sense
only in its fingers of sounds and bays, is conscious
of coasts where the waterbrawn hammers
silence home to men.

But the meaning of silence
he seized for his province, no limp sweet
aesthetic love fondles, no towered lamp illumines,
no promontory of stark thought touches
by too tense sunshine, in too taut a darkness . . .
night, the water roar, the ever wane of the dull wave moan.

South of Point Reyes the ocean belongs
to him.

In it the wreckage of his knowledge,
spars of his hopes, chips of his evening longings
sucked down all and masticated
into the common leaven of worlds.

His slumber
is miles outward beyond the moonswung seabuoy,
where the tourniquet of the slow tide cinches
the simple wound of death.

SONNET

Playing loose with time and love and space,
in one compelling instant you had gone
down down down like a drop of midnight dew
to be dissolved in our bewilderment
when the deathword lay passionless in print
before us and we were unsure we knew
the limits of our Known turning upon
the creaking axle of the commonplace.

Some mouths say this shall not or this must be,
as though the willing would deflect the seeds
from their determination in the mould.
But you did more—shrugged off the growing old
for freedom, scarcely conscious that flesh needs
the consciousness of freedom to be free.

From "OUTLINES"

Three.

The old and imperfect lover fuses
two visions, grooms his innocuous sonnets
by the one hundred watt mazda shower
in his slender bedroom under the stairs.

"O generations, what of love . . . ." he hovers
with light in the thickets of his eyebrows,
loses between the theme and the word
when Mulford stutters on the staircase,
hot from his nightly counsel with cool glasses,

demanding veritable heaven, " What are we here for?
So Carrie itches for the bastard Greek,
the son—" A stubborn Maymoth dazes
the bulb while thought trails under the hand.

What of love basketed in sonnets
as a continuous life recorded
out of the softly drying pulses
into tomorrow into tomorrow and—
Mulford wheezes on the wheeling stairs,

believing, "Another grunt I'll be in heaven
at ten a week. Not bad. Christ cure her body!
The world—" then falters in and finds the button,
stares like death at impure overalls.

AMERICAN PRIMITIVE
Marta (1830-1912)

and Clem her man she survived for twenty years
stand sexless in the funereal frame,
kissed lip-prim by republican Death.
Eyes of the steady American virtues,
trinitarian fork, no fieldnest of dreams
under the furrow driven through iron hair:
her eyes keep all, the all of winter
in eyes with the snowy pastures in them,
Gothic homestead, the goblin bed,
and seventy years of hard Sundays in church,
witnessing to an age going blind.

Our smile is homeless. Regard them, regard
honesty, invisible trumpets announcing
the four-eyed man and his righteous woman
who see as they see, are what they are.
So mortuarized with Once that fringes,
creeps and seeps into necessary Now,
these Ararats in the common disaster

arrest our humble animalless ark
and make us know the miracle of man
simplified in paint with such circumspection
as puzzles the Now zeroed between
ownerless faces and the star-killed sky.

FISHERMEN
You were my lord invincible, made
free play of the woods, bore the patterns of
sunprayer on your shoulders, manly
swung the leaplog path with a
fisherman's stride to the troutspun pool
rocking the audience of woods
by alligator logs asleep
under the antiphonal rays and shadows.

You were my lord of fireweed lancing
noons of light, cocked with brace sure on
stones, quick to the ride of
fly down spawning sibilance where
fat trout dive in the waterlurk,
wavering point to magnetic mountains,
hawkhigh day dappling over
hosanna of treetops, up the greenlift flocking
a spatter of angels on fleetwind to empty sky.

Now you are my lord invisible O
netted in the green life while I fail here
with lips and hands, you in the all of
everything your love cried holy,
toucher and touched remembered as one:
Do you hear now
the willawalla water palavering stream-

stone brokenly over the benches of
fishbed, mountains roaring with sun-
flicked whorls of shine, no universe more
gaily gone than this one?

Arrowing waterlight still, the faulted
heart rare as I
cast this fly for your vivid sake.

OUT OF REACH

What tolls in the mind cannot be written or spoken.

On the wild hill the timber wolf nurses her wild young.
Under the lamp the heart continues itself
in the place of its importance, aware of the wilderness
of lightly surrounding body woven with serviceable blood.

Heart feels the night there, remembers
something, is it a primal age of go-
put-away playthings, kiss of the mother, the
scissored precise geometry of moon
on the stairs of childhood winding upward
to lunar rooms?

What does night mean with its
finger of shadow on the heartsland rising
with gluts of blood, while the shewolf barks
to the moon across the night on the ridge, cries up
to the door of the sleeping house?

What tolls in the mind cannot be written or spoken.

COLOPHON

For C. B.
But for the lovingness
man breaks on beast.
Waters slide away,
and we the simple drowned
wake into swollen bodies
of capable otherselves
guided by the thighs
and the practical kill.

In the shadow of the heart,
where love and folly meet,
crouch and be still.

James B. Hall

DEATH, BY HOT ROD

At midnight what skid or puncture of desire
Dared you race the cams of Time and flame
Your engines out of laughter until the fire
Of speed consumed the brain, and pain
Released the head, now upholstered in the rain?

Is midnight and you drive a road that writhes
And sow the wheel on which the swerve depends,
Rend metal bright as horses scream through sky
And wake the farmer who by telephone can only send
For State Patrol or relay cries to fathers who attend
The flow of oxygen, or puzzle over lights
That were switched off, and hear the Doctor's sigh.

Now, as overcoated men compelled to view our crime
(Or for report) stand marble-footed in this frost
To reconsider, after shock, these ruins chocked in Time:
Of youth whose orbits lay in wheels, who thought
Asteroids could not collide in worlds so lost,
Who can not hear some old garageman from his wrecker say,
"Stand back, men, we got to haul these stripped-down
            wrecks away."

THE HUNT WITHIN

That hill
Is humped raising its weight
Of snows towards the sun
That burns away the high fog and dawn
Of a new mid-winter

41

And the scrub pine
Bristles on that hill's back
Like hackles, while the hound
Digs memory's root of fox dead
Or bone forgotten.

Now the picket
Crow calls black and clarion
Through these encircling woods
And the last dry berry of summer trembles
And drops in moss

While my dog
Grovels the hillock's bluest snow
Whimpering from his forepaw's
Slit tenderness. Now this gun's
Full-primed and

Eager shells
Ram home to their steel chamber
And I want to see
A man crouched or through briars running
To shoot him dead,

Like any game.
Therefore I hunt through sumacs
On the dirty little footprints
Of revenge, and maim even the snipe's
Slack-wing flutter,

Explode the squirrel's
Grey brief and chattering hide,
For vengeance on this land,
Burns, Oh Bloody and firm beneath
This hunting jacket,

Revenge upon
This souring land that made me.
Now the hound claws
The entrails of the hill, the whipping briar
Fires my eye

And the tear
From the thorn and the wind only
Makes course through these hackles
On my cheek, snuffling to answer the ancient
Baying dog, within.

FOUR NECESSARY ENCOUNTERS:

Tortoise

Where hired men bent their backs
Along barbed wire
Across my father's partial soil
Tortoise it was
Old Lee pried from our fence row,
That blue-vine meridian,
When Elm trees blew the fifes of noon.

Tortoise of noon in the sun's shell,
Dated by carving,
Handed me there in the barbed
Wire fences of the sun
That March-day of tenants moving
When all line fences heave
Under the flanks of another Spring.

Tortoise in hand before I knew
Only a tortoise shell
Held farm and fence and the high sullen
Dollar of the sun upon its back,
Dated by carving, and dimly read
In the sun-fenced rows
To a boy's winking, reptile heart.

Snake

Where the briar's rough caress
Begat indignant berries
For our casual harvest,
Where a white-oak stump
Burned in its old slow fire
Of moss, I saw her;

In the center of our woods
Where the lecher briars
Coupled with sumac,
Draping her folds of purple
Scaled-copper against the sky,
Molten and gorged, she slept.

Neither root nor hardpan shuddered
When her slow head
Swayed lewd among leaves
And her sly round reptile eye
Opened, then slowly blinked
Into the face of my trespass;

Old arts forgotten, she bestirred
Her slattern's easy flesh
And roiled across the sumac's roof
Seeking some deeper core of briar
To tell her slack-hide glozing mate
Of guile, seen lately in a boy's eye.

Birds

Lapwing, the deceiver
Or the sneaking jay
A martin, purple
As muscadine
On our twittering vines,
Or the horse-turd sparrow
Wallowed the eye of God;

Peewee, the rain prophet
Or the foraging crow
The quail, harried
By the sun
And the bright hunter's gun,
Or the swallows at nest
Condemned to our barns;

Shikepoke, crane
Or a pigeon suspended
In that Ohio, pagan air:
Each beak pecked its bloody share
And each small worm squealed
In sod, or underneath the locust bark
Courting the old fury of the meadow lark.

Boy

Barbed wire rusts
In a tortoise sun
Beak by briar
May be undone;
What a boy needs know
Need be learned again:
That Winter makes snow,
And Spring makes rain.

IN BAILEY WOODS

Oh young my farmer
Blood and nine, so I leaped
To hear our dogs break the barnyard
Kennels, the limping fox crouched in their eyes,
And Redbone's nostril eager for the split entrails,
In Bailey woods;

Then mother, goodbye!
For somewhere in our swamps
A bitch-fox shudders in her hollow log
While dogs lope through the scrub oak grove,
Answering the horn's throat and following call,
Through Bailey woods.

There nine summers
Stretched their shadow on that cleared
November earth, hearing the bitch-fox
And dogs trailing, until the reeling swamp beneath
My ear's rapt corridor was like a wheel humming
In Bailey woods;

And there in trees
Old Redbone bayed away
His hunting heart, and fell. The fox
Circled, circled that ranging night and trailed
The pack, back-tracked into a reach of Sandy Creek
And there through briars

Watched the dogs
Burry flank and steaming tits
Deep in the slough and sand bars of that
Creek, until they shook the dawn in water spangles
From their wet backs, and lost their trails
In Bailey woods.

Therefore much I
Hunted by patrol, beyond our
Wire into the dark Alsatian nights
Where the flare, slipped by the Very Pistol's throat
Bayed night away, and the Corporal screamed his winter,
In some other woods;

But I am nine
And thirty, now, and want to hear
The hounds' crossed bones bay through the swamp
To rustle the brain's black burnt-out timber land
For once the hunter, bitch, pack and swamps were one,
In Bailey woods.

ON PAY DAY NIGHT

Picture a desert and the *Panzer* man
Goggled even in death by his ruthless
Sun glasses, obeying a last command

To hold a mortar pit though his roofless
Head sucked sand as our platoon
(Aware then only a little of the careless

Sirocco) wondered why—so soon—
Our replacements joined us. But this
Is scarcely remembered, for the loom

Of memory creaks and our old tricks,
Such as those grenades of phosphorus
Tossed scalding into bunkers near Bitche,

Fade nicely; by now it was not us
At all for, like juries, can a platoon
Remember? Happy we are that the rust

Hulk sinks, that Victory is a room
Of some weather station where the godless
Anemometer whines, spinning its doom

By consort with storms. Now, careless
Of policy, we froth this bar with our
Spigot laughter and in darkness caress

The purple flesh of conscience for we are
Old He Ones, so heads I win
A pack of Chesters—and we know The Saar

Is no damned good. Now the gin
And tonics roar for closing time, now
Shall any man forget that day in

Basic that we donned Europe's head, bowed
Into our gas masks and took that gas
Which trained us; saw in a mirror how

Our heads were not bird or fish, or brass
Of Idols, that wagging tube no tongue
To speak, nor beak to shatter glass

For here the goggle, head, and mask were one,
Faceless, no sting, no tear, no sound nor laughter:
We clawed, came out like reptiles—not wise, nor
    young.

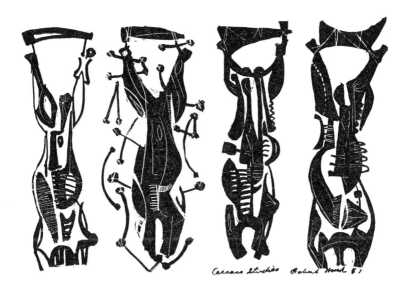

Carcass Studies   Robert Houck 51

Theodore Holmes

SNOWFALL

(after Frost)
A prosperous town had not yet taken
Quite all of the wood
Into which a snow had shaken
The part of the night that it could

This town had grown out of this wood
For as long as its board was able
To furnish a boy with a livelihood
That sat with his fist on the table.

If now the wood seems to be young,
Bother me not to tell
The rich taste on the parent's tongue:
Spoil is one way of getting well.

As for the trees, the tall have beaten
Down on logs the snow that fell;
Whether to cover or more to sweeten,
One wouldn't be lying if one could tell.

A CHRISTMAS CARD

The moon moves just out of reach of the mountain
That rises behind the town like an image of man's desire;
By its light the roofs and steeple of the town look just like
    copies
Of this same image as it is spent with less force.
The moon, in its rising, lifts in the night of our human
    world
The promise of another world,—of which it is the soft
    reflection.

The mountain is the giant shadow it gives rise to and that
　　moves up the valley
Just as the lights are being put out in the houses below,
That dissolves the roofs in the darkness of a completer
　　oblivion
Before the return of the little consciousness moonlight
　　allows:
It is the moon that sets the stars in the frost on the
　　windowpane.

In this town, snuggled tightly beneath their blankets,
With the mountain now as only some dark outline in the
　　head,
The people go over their shopping trips in preparation for
　　the season's joy;
Christmas is the season of the sacrifice each makes
Toward the day when, in ribbons and bows, he will feel the
　　Easter of his joy.
With prayers on his lips and in the garden of the charity
　　in his heart,
Each hopes, alone in the dumbness of his thoughts,
That his hands contain the gifts another will be grateful to
　　him for;
In bed, he passes again the crowds of people he hardly knows
　　with packages on the street,
Walking before the windows which, no matter how much
　　we buy, we never seem able to touch;
Walking before the signs which the season seems especially
　　proud of:
Hire the handicapped; it is good business. He feels himself
　　jostled by the crowds
Turning up the streets, climbing the hills of their giving,
That makes them feel easier by what each Christmas con-
　　tains of the first,

When as children in their beds they knew that everything
    below was theirs;
As they mill through the stores looking for someone's drop
    of blood
That they can make their own, filling the wooden crosses of
    the aisles with their feet,—
Their arms like the branches of the trees killed to make
    the floor,
He feels each reach made to test the vessel they have come
    to carry their giving in:
A shawl for grandmother, a pair of the sheerest stockings
    for mother,
A doll for Dottie that closes her eyes when you lay her down
    to sleep;
For junior a soldier with tin eyes and a pop-gun that shoots
    us dead.
Christmas is the time we put flesh on our loves—
As when in bed on a Winter night we turn to our warmth
With the only present that our flesh is sacrifice enough for,
And the busy city streets dance with produce in our veins.

Outside of the sleeper's room, inside the arms in which he
    has fallen to sleep,
The moon slides past and the stars come out behind it
From the darkness that closes in the human search for each
    other at night;
The stars that have been hidden by the shining of this
    nearer light—
And out of all this heavenly host, three wise men once
Needed only one to guide them to the crib of regenerate
    man.

AN ARTIST DESCRIBES THE SYMPHONY

"A symphony is like all other works of art:
At first restless on a bed of ancient springs
Trying to get to sleep; everywhere at once
Guts and valves refining the supper lump,
Each tuning to his own dinner needs.

"Just as the early imagoes of sleep arise
From the scrap of something swallowed whole
Consciously demanding an unconscious order,
The patrons begin to turn the aisles
From ticket agencies into life; if only
These could get where they are going
Without the action needed for their coming;
This army of occupying appetite
In which music raises a hiccup of sense.
Finally, a measure of its medium, the song begins
To transcribe the silent running score
On the held out pages of interpreting faces,
Composed by sleep that is almost perfect
Harmony between movement and life; sleep,
The equilibrium between food and feces.
And so music is an arrangement to hold
The performance of a body at its stunt
With the promise after of escaping hunger.

"The doors will open on nothing visibly chaned;
The people faced hard as ever with the fact,
To eat fast is a slow change; the desire
To get at what life is really like will leave
The hall dark, the program upon the floor."

THE DOE

(For Jamie Smart)
A locust stillness hung;
The noon's breathless breath
Filled the wild Gethsemane
With lilting radiance and calm.
Green blade's touch upon my neck,
Eyes traveled the present
Heavy root to sinuous extremities beyond
Lost in the foreign frolic
Of their cool commingled shades.

The lit fuse burnt, betrayed
An intruder rude till I turned
On mute suspended fear; poised naked.
Her tan flesh shrinking thighward
As the proud self-conscious Eve
First to our first progenitor appeared,
Stood across her wooded threshold
A virgin deer.

Royalty, kindness, love and fear
Her pulse beat (the bow tensely
Drawn holds the quivering chord).
Alone, she bodied all her life;
The vine about the limb, the fallen leaf,
The loud heart huddled in the brush and
Beyond; all crowned there in her eyes.

Our gaze transfixed; there hung unasked
The eternal, unanswered question:
Does she wonder at my wonder or want
Me, as her slave, her own; Yes! I'll go—
But at my move she moved away
Into her echoing advent growing gray.
This day yet I see her eyes;
Soft, tearless, their treasure locked.

WAITING FOR THE BUS

The hills slope away from us like prayers
Toward clouds set out on the horizon like fresh bread;
The sun that is strong overhead
Leaves a spot before our eyes.

As men, standing under the tree of our aspiration,
We watch the birds fly, papers fly, and the leaves fly,
For we know that their trying to climb
Is trying to climb the mountain that is smooth within us,
And that the suitcases at the end of the trip
Contain all that we had with us. Thought?
It can be seen on any street corner:
It has a waiting face.

A WORKING GIRL

(after seeing her first Toulouse-Lautrec)
"Each hour I am out to lunch
Here in this terminus of a man's world,
I stand above the roadbed a heel's height
At the intersection where two streets meet.
Behind me and before me are the licked meat
Posters of what I can barely afford to buy

With what I get my weekly wages in;
These sticker store-fronts composed by man
Of whatever it is that I am made without
Contract me like a dream, by what it spoils:
A trinket made to dangle on the crib of wish.
All my waking is a waking to sleep
Memory encountered on these easels of price;
A sleep I know hides someone else's tongue
Behind the gummed label of my appetite.
And so I love my work just as automobiles
That pass here seem to meet
Without ever bumping or jamming up the street
Even as they close into that farther corner
Which never seems to fill and less seems to retreat;
An anterior knowledge in the driver's seat.
I wish I had before me the paint and brush
To paint the picture without my own self in
The picture I've been drawing wages in. But I forget:
Each day I use a nickel lipstick too well
To scribble down the passionate particulars
The way I please.

         Another way would have been
The life of ease;

           all those manly ads women
Leave unopened until their lips have sealed
The acceptance their cradle will be suckled in;
Before they ever go out to lunch. They must tire
Meeting on street corners only the need
To get their car across; in the windows the signs
Being always only what they labor to say
They've already got at home. This I think tells

The difference between a married girl and me,
Is the married difference of the degree
Of their admission. We both make a living,
But I make mine where it is not given
To be the chauffeur of my shopping trips."

A SCHOLAR'S CHRISTMAS VACATION

It is spent like a toy soldier
Running out in himself a coil of breath
Until the spring, going inside,
Comes loosely to require his death.

The first hurry is to buy replies
To all the open invitations one spends
One's life trying satisfactorily to fill:
Gifts to stuff the season's open ends.

Christmas Day is all the greeting
Piled beside the mask of open gifts;
The spent expectancy of waiting
Is more than all, a plundering of ifs.

It is the part that the year has left,
To wait and not expect, that finishes
What the blowing of a toy balloon begins
To make the chest feel as it diminishes.

Since this week, you have smelled life out
As the requirement for gift; since death
Is what the Old couldn't put off for a year,
You greet the New with your nose to its breath.

Sandgren
El Gitano

Ernest G. Moll

WINTER PLOUGHING

This morning after my plough
Starlings streamed and chattered
Shimmering green, and now
Suddenly gold-bespattered.

And a mudlark and his mate,
Bright on the winter ground,
Delicate, prim, sedate,
Followed me round on round.

And one black crow was there
Pulling worms from their burrow
With his solemn courtly air
Busy along the furrow.

And joy was mine though I knew
The roots must die that I bared;
And beetle and grub were few
The crow and the starling spared.

For the birds with tug and nod
Dealt death for the need of their lives,
And my coulters in the sod
Were shining and sharp as knives.

KOOKABURRAS

I've heard the skylark Shelley heard,
The ruffled thrush that Hardy knew,
The English nightingale that stirred
The dying heart of Keats when dew
Silvered the moonlit lawns where he
Had left so little time to be.

I've heard the wren in rocky glades
Darting his silver lance of sound,
And high among the white Cascades
The purple finch pour, round on round,
Fire-music that should swirl and swing
And loose the torrents of the spring.

And all of these with joy or pain
Were lyrical, as though they wrought
In sunshine or in slanting rain
To free some urgent hidden thought
Whose brightness man at last should see
On the dark brows of Tragedy.

But kookaburras when the west
Burns red behind the ringbarked trees,
And the dark earth sinks down to rest
And every flower has lost its bees,
Shake the still dusk with sudden mirth
Flung recklessly across the earth.

In gusts of sound their laughter breaks
Against the steepening walls of night
And listening then my spirit takes
Backward through time the wings of flight
And hears among the ghosts at play
The lusty laugh of Rabelais.

BOTTLE SWALLOWS

They built beneath the hanging banks
Along the creek. Their nests of brown
Stiff clay in colonies and ranks
Were like rough gourds with necks turned down.

I'd sit and watch the mother birds
Slip in and out; a thousand wings
And a great festival of words
That must have stood for happy things.

But now and then a sparrow came,
Bluff-shouldered pirate, for a nest,
Truculent, without song or shame
Or spot of fear within his breast.

The swallows never drove him off
But seemed to mark, from stone and limb,
Attentively to hear him scoff
At all that they might do to him.

And, seeming pleased to have them there,
Meek victims of his easy sin,
He'd jerk his head with scornful air
And choose his nest and enter in.

Then came what I had known would come:
The swallows left on wings as still,
As soundless as an unbeaten drum
Or sudden shadow on a hill.

And in a moment they were back,
Hundreds with little bits of clay
To seal the robber in and pack
Him down for ever from the day.

It took not longer than a minute;
And then the swallows far and near
Said over something that had in it
What seemed like laughter to my ear.

Another tomb among the many
Blind, awful mouths already there!
But thinking pleasant thoughts, if any,
I went about my own affair.

My own affairs I'm bent on still,
But now in me the twitterings run
Where sudden wing and clever bill
Shut something in against the sun.

Blind mouths! Ah God, if I could get
Clear of the accusing memory
That I broke never a nest to let
A single panting sparrow free!

HOLD DEAR THINGS NOT TOO CLOSE

Hold dear things not too close
But touch them lightly so
That when their moment goes
They, too, may go
With never a scar to tell
How once you loved them well.

And let not dear things bide
Too long against your heart;
But wisely all provide
That your parting, when you part,
Be not as flesh from bone
But as water slipping from stone.

SPIDER

(Fable of a Neurosis)
As spiders go, he was more civilized
Than most, and strung his web a little tighter,
With knot and brace more cunningly devised
To take the strain, because his thread was lighter.

Sportsman by instinct, connoisseur in taste,
He had no interest in the vulgar fly
And shunned the forthright beetle in his haste
To find some dung before it should be dry.

But for the veined ephemera of the night,
The wandering psyches wonderful and pale,
He had a lust as hunger-hammered and bright
As the hard metal of some savage grail.

Hunting was good, but since the victims were
Nearly all wing, there was no juice to press;
The hunter kept on saying, "These I prefer,"
And grew the gaunter on his own success.

At last he ate them only with his eyes.
To compensate his belly with the thrill
Their struggling made along the spokes and guys,
He pulled the web a little tighter still.

Just when he'd half convinced himself that soon
The Incomparable would strike his web, it did:
Something fell on him from the capsized moon
And ended dream and web and arachnid.

Yet not quite dead, he lies on the cold ground
Crushed by a butterfly that opens and shuts
Enormous wings and smothers him, bound
By the silver cordage of his very guts.

WIFE TO A SECOND HUSBAND

Take valley, hill and meadows
They're yours by title clear,
And try to understand
When silently as shadows
The big-eyed gentle deer
Refuse your proffered hand.

AFTER THE FIRE

Walk with me, then, but keep
Your eyes hard as stone;
What has died here will sleep
Better if left alone.

That blackened stump is not
Your tree of pleasant airs;
Pass him, gaunt, grim and squat,
Minding his own affairs.

That burnt heap with a thong,
The pet-lamb you called Queen?
Rubbish! but come along,
The rain makes dead bones clean!

Here was your garden—here?
No! but don't look again;
The grass waits spear on spear
The first drums of the rain.

Better come on; this place
Has done with you—its choice!
Has turned away its face
And stopped its ears to your voice.

THRIFT

He loved his horse; and when it died
Grabbed his knife and got its hide.
The cash—consider while you praise—
Kept him drunk for seven days.

RED CHARLIE

Red Charlie had seen wars and sin
And killed his men—he'd tell about them—
"I wonder what their hats," he'd grin,
"Will do without them."

We knew him hard and thought him worse,
And often we would tell each other,
"Charlie would tipple in a hearse
Or stab his brother."

When Toby lost his teeth and grew
So frail even Charlie wouldn't boot him.
One noon we made up lots and drew
To see who'd shoot him.

The lot was Charlie's. With a word
That froze the rising run of laughter,
He turned, and Toby slowly stirred
And trotted after

To live for years blind, deaf, and fat,
With Charlie by to feed and tend him;
Charlie, who'd emptied many a hat,
And couldn't end him.

Robert Krieger

THE DELAY

When I struggled out from your final hold
Into the orchard's intractable air, what wild
Willingness to stay sprang at my head
On that planked road caving to the sea?

Then did you appeal, and your bees
In lively invitation danced to tell
The colors of goodbye, their pollen dropping
Dark on the long way down the rock.

But my ship rolled too, its figurehead
Crying the real predicament, the sea!
And still I lolled, cold for separation,
While all the winds moved slowly round.

Love, was there no sign for relenting?
And when it came, that backward-driven gull,
Blinded and old, silent with regrets,
What sent him soaring wrong through furious air?

For all my favorite joy the ropes held fast;
The wind that turned the gull turned me,
Who, whirling, saw orchards break at the cliff,
Saw, for the first time, new foam in the branches.

ELK

Heard him take his running in the wood
And hooves strike winter from a buried bell;
Where long branches hung with ice
Six antlers sprang; before the moon
Another six, and held against a single fir
He stood, legs set to cold again,
And fled, his keen cloved feet afire,
His head twelve-tined like a running year.

69

APPEARANCES

Even the gulls cry water's dominion;
From tidal-flats over outcropped, shining beaches
Dunes shift inland. Ever to eastward
Angles drift as high as the sand-tops lie;
Where rhododendrons, burning in a slough, blow to be
    buried,
Direction binds longing and distance together.

Between Cape Blanco and unsighted forests
I, a bicycle, and a ten-mile country of dunes
Are moving scenery to the wind's persistence.
In a haze of flutters, the eye holds nothing;
Wheels turn and grind back
Endless sandscape in a kind of silence.

Even the gulls drop like a question,
Dimming half our sky; old grass goes blind.
If choiceless winds never turn, our face set homeward,
The wheels' direction is our only keeping.
Riding, riding, the bicycle makes small distance.

NIGHT AT THE FISH TRAPS

Smoking as a spell, old as rock
At the edge of pilings near the wickerwork traps,
Townswomen do not heed this slow talk
Of water on ropes. It is the young girls
Who feel its deft weight, its hazy story,
Its pebble-voice rolled deep at the river-bed.
They peer; their eyes polish such darkness.
But women, intractable, have always said,
"Water has never entered like a wave
Nor whispered anything to us."

70

Still the young must leap to its net.
Tonight, townswomen know, girls will cry
Between the lean and fat of their wisdom,
Trying hard to grow old in it.

A NOW FAMOUS ESCAPE

> "I float in that balloon over myself
> Seeing my own darkness in the light."
> Casimir Wierzynski

The ropes that held its wonder swayed;
I felt my body move through airy tides
Above each head, above the maypoled firs
And pylons, rising above this country-fair
(The pulleys creaked, the harness flew) ,
And lifted from such bondage at midday,
I left my elders looking up.
Wind whirled the lines and I was canopied.
Arise, arise sang all my breath
Ascending voiceless in that wild balloon
Past fells of sky, above their silent death,
Drifting where clouds blew light itself.
I had no weight, I swooned;
I dreamed a voice flew in a rage
Sighing and sighing up is down;
I woke. What winds can bear this load?
And as I fell, unsettled from my hold,
My elders' hands rose high to greet me,
For they had never loosed the silken ties.
And then like one who falls
And turns to look the crowd apart,
I heard a rumor running everywhere:
My adversary cried, my murdering self,
"Goodbye loud sun, goodbye sweet answering air!"

71

CHILD ON A PULLMAN

Such privilege was his—to stay bewitched
And ride those sundown rails above the world!
But the furious train, passing each right-of-way,
Outsteps his map, each friendly look

And suddenly transforms its character,
Leaps flat on wheels round a slickered hill.
Derelict, he rocks at twilight now,
A face in a cloud of hopelessness.

No doors open down the unmarked plains,
Through fog the engine hammers, in dark he haunts.
He keeps his fear: wheels forget and slow;
Glass rattles twice and he is nowhere.

Falsity of hello, hello and good-evening
Greets him under a station's warping sign
Where endlessly trailed by unaccountable baggage,
He turns, he sets his face toward home,

For what he finds leaps heavy at each door,
A draft at corners pounces for his breath;
Here nothing cries reprieve, the bells beat back,
Ringing such loss he cannot hold.

HOMECOMING

Now when I came, still anxious for my kin,
I did not walk an easy way that night.
All the dry leaves that thronged the air
Drifted to my astonishment.

Woodsmoke I remembered, and grass deepening
A ruined wall. But where I turned, before
Me then, the flash of ordinary things
Was half at odds, the stones unsure.

Silence and no-one. I stepped beside that door.
Only my shadow swung upon the sill;
How might I face them, those loves spent foolishly,
Each privilege loosened like a girl?

Half to myself I knocked, half to myself,
And every sound rose echoing through the rooms—
Not name, no bell, but an old dog barking
From emptiness as from a dream.

MY LIFE, MY DEATH

His body stillborn, sent packing with death
Down perilous avenues I must take,
He runs from me from the darkness of our birth,
My brother, my double, my long-lost twin.

And where shall I find him, freed by fate
To a life under his personal cloud?
Born seconds later, where shall I find him
Brushing the naked webs of fear?

My brother never speaks nor does—
He flees, a crumpled hand upon his mouth;
And I must follow him, climb up the stairs
To be affronted by a face.

What is the image that I see,
Hands tapping glass my own look countermands?
"Brother," I cry, and hear a cold voice call,
"There is not blood enough for two!"

They say one twin must harm the other—
My lawless brother murders me
Making my life mean death, my love shoot hate.
Two men, two individual men we were

But guilt, eternal knee upon my chest,
False surgeon of a thread has made us one
And where my brother's footsteps go,
In shadowing him I lose myself.

"Brother," I ask him as I must,
"Is there no place we both may meet,
The living and the comrade-dead,
To break the crystal of my plight?"

I beg him solve this travesty
That from the womb still robs me of my life,
Commend me to his self-content,
Who claps my future in his hands—

And there, where both our selves
Stand undefended in the light,
Let me, one furtive moment in his smile,
See my forgiveness and his love.

IN THE TIDE PONDS

The ponds, that summer afternoon, showed
No wild comfort—we waited by their side.
Though we had hoped for little more than this,
The grass sank deep as beds, and inshore rode
A helmsman-bird, rare and sulphurous.

Each flower stood for cutting then, a broil
Of color rocking in a cloudless sway.
Water kept its full; there was no flow
But happiness, so heart took half, and soon
Assured of wherewithal, gave half away.

And visibly, skyward from our hills,
The resinous forests burned the air to blue;
Weeds spilled their catch of ragged fruit
As if asleep, and so our old regrets
Fell ignorant as many hours turned,

Until the spell of waywardness flew off,
Until, at peace, we let the journey go,
And like a promise laid upon our ears
Heard, first at the water's edge, "Sleep well,
You will not hunger in this country-side."

FLOWERING ANTLER

Met at the entrance of this wood,
Lover with lover, lost with lost,
How shall we tell each other what it means
Who are not satisfied to call it horn,
Buck's horn, but what we make of it.

It is of beast for good or ill
And eyes can mark such bone as kin,
Deep-rooted as the mind's old grudge;
It is of sweat, and animal, a chiseled
Wood sprung wild against the world.

How may our breath hold back, our love
Not claim this bough a dazzling gift?
Tines burn and silver by the fire
Or at our touch—a scented shield
His shagged and open head foreswore.

And do we need to say what pain
Occurred, how he ran breathless from this wood,
Brute hold torn finally away,
Or how he flung this specter by,
Dark bane his loving self redeemed?

We need not draw the telling out,
For all its windings are the same,
And in its rise and willful fall
Lie our mind's flame, and our mind's chill
That sets the smiling in your look

And weaves its story into ours
While beasts run freely in this wood;
Twelve-tined, it stands and burns and blooms;
It points us to our pledge, fires
Lover homeward, lost to lost.

William E. Stafford

THE OLD SCOUT

Holding heretical ideas about non-controversial subjects
this unnoticeable genius disappeared
off there in a bend of the West, in Oregon light
where many a dim cabin brought the slur of old age to him.

With his habit of wandering strengthened by hunger,
he could climb farther than we can see.
He worked the steel trap; it often failed,
but all that he caught he preserved in bear grease.

Now that horns of our herd are so politically employed,
harmlessly we too may be original.
Think about him: his kind of politics,
just glancing at the sky when he got up in the morning.

THINGS WE DID THAT MEANT SOMETHING

Thin as memory to a bloodhound's nose,
being the wedge of some new knowing,
I often glance at a winter color—
husk or stalk, a sunlight touch,
maybe a wasp nest in the brush
near the winter river with silt like silver.

Once with a slingshot I hit a wasp nest:—
without direction but sure of right,
released from belief and into act,
hornets planed off by their sincere faith.
Vehement response for them was enough,
patrolling my head with its thought like a moth:—

"Sometime the world may be hit like this
or I getting lost may walk toward this color
far in old sunlight with no trace at all,
till only the grass will know I fall."

79

HOLDING THE SKY

We saw a town by the track in Colorado.
Cedar trees below had sifted the air,
snow water foamed the torn river there,
and a lost road went climbing the slope like a ladder.

We were traveling between a mountain and Thursday,
holding pages back on the calendar,
remembering every turn in the roadway:
we could hold that sky, we said, and remember.

On the western slope we crashed into Thursday.
"So long," you said when the train stopped there.
Snow was falling, touching in the air.
Those dark mountains have never wavered.

DOUBT ON THE GREAT DIVIDE

One of the lies the world is compelled to tell
is that God grips boards by thought into Plato's table.
Better to stand in the dark of things and crash,
hark yourself, blink in the day, eat bitter bush
and look out over the world. A steadfast wire
shaking off birds into the paralyzed air
crosses the country; in the sound of noon you stand
while tethers whisper out and come to their end.

Mountains that thundered promises now say something
       small—
wire in the wind, and snow beginning to fall.

THE RESEARCH TEAM IN THE MOUNTAINS

We have found a certain heavy kind of wolf.
Haven't seen it, though—
just *know* it.

80

Answers are just echoes, they say. But
a question travels before it comes back,
and that counts.

Did you know that here everything is free?
We've found days that wouldn't allow a price
on anything.

When a dirty river and a clean river
come together the result is—
dirty river.

If your policy is to be friends in the mountains
a rock falls on you: the only real friends—
you can't help it.

Many go home having "conquered a mountain"—
they leave their names at the top in a jar
for snow to remember.

Looking out over the campfire at night
again this year I pick a storm for you,
again the first one.

We climbed Lostine and Hurricane and Chief Joseph
        canyons;
finally in every canyon the road ends.
Above that—storms of stone.

AT THE SORTING ROOM

Tonight sorting old clothes for the poor
I held the sleeve of a brown sweater.
That yarn ran wrinkling a moment—
Mother was opening the door—
it was knitted far from here.

81

On the ceiling of the room a light bulb twittered—
Mother wore brown, her hair was like a hood;
her face looked white when it turned toward me—
in how calm loops that sleeve was knitted!
It would last a lifetime; the weave was good.

The poor are with us, are everywhere,
a needy, a wide-eyed, a hungry race;
I folded for them the old brown sweater,
but I stopped a minute at the open drawer
and smoothed with my hand in the empty place.

BEFORE THE BIG STORM

You are famous in my mind.
When anyone mentions your name
all the boxes marked "1930's"
fall off the shelves;
And the orators on the Fourth of July
all begin shouting again.
The audience of our high school commencement
begin to look out of the windows at the big storm.

And I think of you in our play—
oh, helpless and lonely!—crying,
and your father is dead again.
He was drunk; he fell.

When they mention your name,
our houses out there in the wind
creak again in the storm;
And I lean from our play, wherever I am,
to you, quiet at the edge of that town:
"All the world is blowing away."
"It is almost daylight."
"Are you warm?"

82

REQUIEM

Mother is gone. Bird songs wouldn't let her breathe.
The skating bug broke through the eternal veil.
A tree in the forest fell; the air remembered.
Two rocks clinked in the night to signal some meaning.

Traveler north, beyond where you can return,
hearing above you the last of the razor birds whizz
over the drift of dust that bore your name,
there's a kind of waiting you teach us—the art of not
    knowing.

Suicidal gestures of nobility driven to the wrist,
our molten bodies remembering some easier form,
we feel the bones assert the rites of yesterday
and the flow of angular events becoming destiny.

Summer and locusts own the elm part of town;
on the millpond moss is making its cream.
Our duty is just a certain high kind of waiting;
beyond our hearing is the hearing of the community.

FOR THE GRAVE OF DANIEL BOONE

The farther he went the farther home grew.
Kentucky became another room;
the mansion arched over the Mississippi;
flowers were spread all over the floor.
He traced ahead a deepening home,
and better, with goldenrod:

Leaving the snakeskin of place after place,
going on—after the trees
the grass, a bird flying after a song.
Rifle so level, sighting so well
his picture freezes down to now,
a story-picture for children.

They go over the velvet falls
into the tapestry of his time,
heirs to the landscape, feeling no jar:
it is like evening; they are the quail
surrounding his fire, coming in for the kill;
their little feet move sacred sand.

Children, we live a barb-wire time
but like to follow the old hands back—
the ring in the light, the knuckle, the palm,
all the way to Daniel Boone,
hunting our own kind of deepening home.
From the land that was his I heft this rock.

Here on his grave I put it down.

FALL JOURNEY

Evening came, a paw, to the gray hut by the river.
Pushing the door with a stick, I opened it.
Only a long walk had brought me there,
steps into the continent they had placed before me.

I read weathered logs, stone fireplace, broken chair,
the dead grass outside under the cottonwood tree—
and it all stared back. We've met before, my memory
started to say, somewhere . . .

And then I stopped: my father's eyes were gray.

AT THE CUSTER MONUMENT

They buried the soldiers where they fell;
their markers go sudden and white.
In the valley of the Little Big Horn
history explodes into quiet.

"While the grass grows the land is yours."
But gold brought in the miners,
and Custer was pushed toward Crazy Horse,
to a meeting this grass remembers.

The wounded cried "Water!" all afternoon.
Spilling down the hillside
go scattered markers of volunteers
who tried for the river that night.

Where Crazy Horse rode like a flung war bonnet
fluttering at the white man,
truing the grass a low wind cuts
through the valley of the Little Big Horn.

PICKING UP CHORES
Picking up chores the first fall day,
pocketing plenty of change, sun dimes,
I trample, then stand on the drying hay.

Clear through the morning high in the throat
on the scheduled wind where the milkweed came
a train is crying for timberline.

Geese flying over the history of summer
yelp to laggards their high lost note;
the wind sounds old over dying hay.

I could let sagebrush buy my farm,
improve the land with its cautious green,
and it all go quiet as the train has gone . . .

I stare toward winter through the first fall day.

John E. Bellamy

STRAIGHT MAN

In his own way he went straight; he had no gift
For dexterous indirection of the mind's storm,
Confining within the geometry of form
Urges unshaped and aching for their drift.
All grievances, hatreds, all unhappiness,
All that a hostile world could do to stress
That he had prime material for expression,
Translated straightway into violence.
He lunged headlong towards early recognition:
A man whose guts were straighter than his sense,
Straight man to the round world's devious merriment.
Making his move too soon to be a sensation,
He quickly fell; his sole identification
The artful swirling of his fingerprint.

AFTERWARDS

Afterwards, the straightened gut-strings sag.
Silence, void of atoms, fills the void.
Oh, God, the quietness, the quietness
That is abroad!

No puns now, now no space for cleverness;
Only an empty space her lovely head—
How cruelly language hastens to my cause
When her love's dead!

NEW MEXICO IN RETROSPECT

Thrown on the clouded retina of the mind
The piled-up ash heaps and the cinder cones,
Like that bleak dump over which the staring eye
Of Dr. Eckleburg watched ceaselessly,
Become the purple mountains' majesty;

While the pitiless gaze of everlasting noon
Relents, and the tattle-tale-gray cotton fields
Fathered and midwived by the gasping wells
From the lank loins of the laboring sand
Seem set amid magnolia and moss.
Around each grain of sand a pearly tear,
On the watery, bleary retina of the mind.

THE HEART OF THE MATTER

That Beatrice, by Tuscan Dante loved,
Who through his magic numbers was assigned
The station of a petal in God's rose,
Was flesh and bones and blood-filled womankind.

The lady Laura, she whom Petrarch fed
By rimes umbilical, and brought to birth
A green-appareled sonnet, had, no doubt,
A rude solidity, and weight and girth.

And each ethereal lady courtly loved
And stoppered in a castle, certainly
Displaced her scented water when she bathed
With mass of measurable density.

The stuff has vanished, while the dreams remain;
But squinting back along the misty ways,
Historians of the dream must contemplate
Some weighty matter bulking in the haze.

ON PICASSO'S PIERROT

Light spills down the middle of the face
To splash into the splendor of the ruff.
One eye catches a moist gleam, the other
Marks a vacant aperture. An empty space
Is the staring nostril, and the open mouth
Black with no bone showing. The skull-
Cap is oddly foreshortened under the wrap-around
Hat which seems to rest, not on the skull,
But on something insubstantial between.
The right hand also insubstantial:
Not drawn, suggested, infinitely obscene,
Livid and jagged, like the crags of hell.

LYELL'S *PRINCIPLES OF GEOLOGY*

Not flood, he said, nor rude catastrophe,
But gentle winds that blew from day to day
And drops of water dropping endlessly;
Creation, said Lyell, came about this way.
No tempests tearing features in great shocks,
No torrents gouging maps in six-day shifts:
Only the tap of water on the rocks,
Only the whisper of breezes on the cliffs.
And no one around even to be lulled to sleep,
As he would have been, not knowing how earth-shaping
An event was taking place. On the face of the deep
No expression. On land not even creatures creeping.
It must have been rather disappointing for God,
After the task, to have no one here to applaud.

THE MISANTHROPE

He assumes the cramped position in a box,
Or stands with legs apart watching the moles
From the vantage point of a molehill,
Holding his belly at the sight of holes

Raised up by inquisitive but wary noses;
Or in an outhouse analyzing feces
Composes in excremental agony
His misanthropic theses.

Swift had reason for a measuring rod
And Queen Anne's Tory ministers' adulation,
And a cosmos that unconditionally guaranteed
A comfortable system of subordination.

Reason deserted him, politics did him wrong,
His world-view left him lower on the Chain
Than whinnying beasts of burden; and he made
Disgust his religion, scatology his fane.

Henry Mencken, after his happy days,
Trampled on an awkward nation's face
With hob-nailed sesquipedalian adjectives
And howled in eloquent merriment at the trace

Of his sharp spikes, then for his manifold sins
Condemned to languish in a middle state:
Painfully poised on the lip, the saliva of mirth
Must have become the bitter spittle of hate.

Mark Twain could chart the Mississippi's bends
And chain the horsepower of the paddle wheel,
But ran aground on economic shoals,
And the hard facts of currency raked his keel.

So crablike crawled back into boyhood and
Thence back into the womb, and found things there
Dark and gloomy (as he should have known),
Then came out blinking in the sun's wide stare

Blinded to the world as to the womb,
And sought a meta-solipsist oblivion.
There is no God, no world, no race, no life,
No heaven and no hell, was his religion.

Yet Swift loved Stella, Tom and Dick and Harry;
No better friend than Mencken could be found
Is what the news from Baltimore attests,
And friendship tracked Sam Clemens like a hound.

In a time of Peale and Carnegie (D., not A.),
When hearts are worn on upreared buttocks, we
Might notice that they also in their way
Display a positive hypocrisy.

SOME MISCONCEPTIONS IN GREEK MYTHOLOGY

The Attic Hecataeus, scientist,
Criticized the Grecian dramatist
For making foolish and misleading claims
About the celestial sport of certain dames
Who attributed the paternity of their issues
To Apollo, or Poseidon, or to Zeus.
He had no doubts about Achilles' birth,
But reckoned his conception nearer earth.
To Hecataeus, those literary freaks,
The heroes of the stories of the Greeks,
Were terrestrial, natural, phenomenal,
Not heroes, but just bastards after all.

91

The central fact, as anyone should see,
Was not transcendence, but adultery.
The issue, then (or question, to be fair),
Was whether conception took place in mid air
Or under. Hecataeus never found
That gods can fashion heroes on the ground.

THE POWER OF SYMPATHY

An old, lone woman knows her loneliness best
From dusk to bedtime, when the necessary work
And what she has invented no longer serve
To shut it out. That time is loneliest.
And we who view the scene from out of doors
Scream in our hearts in sudden sympathy.
An old, lone woman's loneliness can be
Bounded by the history of her woes:
The annals of her old exile provide
Acquaintance with the hard terms of her fate
And knowledge of the geography of her fears.
Sympathy is a mad shriek at eventide;
Sounded from dusk to bedtime it could shout
Down every lonely house about our ears.

COLLEGE STUDENT

His mind snaps shut upon a single phrase,
And his opinion is indeed his own,
And will remain so, unchallenged and alone.

In the market place of ideas he is a miser,
With little prospect of becoming wiser,
Or wealthier in good coin. He seeks no praise,
But only safety. How did this come about?
How has he learned so well to do without
In an economy so full that even fool's gold
Is legal tender where minds are bought and sold?
Has he sold everything for this soft self-praise?

What seems sometimes strange is that his age
Has made the committee and conference the rage.
One would think these meetings of the group
Would teach the stiff, unbending mind to stoop
To recognition of a neighbor's phrase.
But logic, syntax, hard consistencies,
Weigh little in the new consistories;
The fashionable mind is pristine, insular.
Wrapped in each constellation every star
(Light miles of dark between) in luminous praise.

COME, LOVELY AND SOOTHING DEATH

Asprawl in the corridor,
(Bulged bricks, line-squared
Squeezed down the distance
Where eye presses masses in) ;
Asprawl, all extremities
Outflung like snapped springs
From the limp center;
Asprawl, what was cellular
Now indivisible
(What was peninsular
Now become insular) ;
He lies in the alleyway.

Light from the street is shed
Bleak in his honor:
Fire without flicker,
Flame without warmth
Fix his indignity.

In mocking mourning the
Street noises sing to him.

COLD COUNTRY BALLAD

"Daughter O daughter, my hand moves the cradle,
And what shall I give you at christening?"

"A tear, a pearl, and a circle of cool,
With these I am rich in beginning."

"Daughter O daughter, my hand twines the wreath,
What shall I give you when men leave you weeping?"

"More than all the young men will be reaping,
A tear, a pearl, and a circle of cool."

"Daughter O daughter, my hand at your brow,
What can I give you to lighten the birthing?"

"A tear, a pearl, and a circle of cool,
Soon it is over and I shall be resting."

"Daughter O daughter, my hand seeks the lamp
What will you take with you darkly retreating?"

"With these I am shrived of my sinning,
A tear, a pearl, and a circle of cool."

"Daughter O daughter, my hand sews the shroud
For what will you know in your sleeping?"

"A tear, a pearl, and a circle of cool,
All of life's worth in having and keeping."

FIREWEED

Sprouting its name the lance-like leaves
Start slow and mild as milk
But thrust to six-foot height on torches,
Magenta, flagged in silk,
Which summer long run blossom-riot

Over blighted land
And waste laid by an element
Got out of human hand,
Till fall when swaying flares bloom down
To embered seed and coal;
When, as if doused, they blow in clouds,
In puffs of drifting wool.

ON LOOKING TOO LONG INTO A CERTAIN BOOK

Who missionaries to a Lapp should know
The flock-and-shepherd talk will prove too deep;
His metaphor is meaningless in snow
Where congregation's never seen a sheep.

He'd best adapt the tilting of his words
To action, hunt his way around the ear;
In countries where the people stalk their herds
One whispers his persuasion with a spear.

And so in my snowbound polarity,
With patience shortened and the time on ration,
While much impressed by ambiguity,

I'd nod less in the churches that you fashion,
(Remember what you said, you build for me)
If you'd forego the text and preach the passion.

POSTCARDS FROM SCAPPOOSE
I.
So far so near to find
The likeliness in our unlikelihood.
Stopped here for coffee and it's fresh.
They have an airport. Down the line
A piece, a man has made his fortune
Farming hair on heads. A notice
States their Indians will scalp all comers
Come football.

II.
Yes, thank you, black. Would seem
There's more than meets the casual eye in cow
And log economy. Their schools
Sport paint. Side streets are french-heel deep
In gravel. Man who filled the tank here
Raises orchids as a hobby.
So the sought at length at hand . . . . We must be
Pushing on.

OLD FISHSTATION

Leans half to river, lurches half to dike—
And both have come with claws.
Mud blocks the door. The sign has drifted off.
Who will tell the traveler what it was?
Only a native remembers when all the business
Here was catch: the smallcraft swarms that stormed
The hive, the robber-trucks that took the treasure inland.
Pier-reach, shifting gangways crusted in brilliance,
Rungs that led both down and up with gleaming
Indifference—they are one with water and the wind.

Soon too the simplified shell will go
Floating and fouling the nets, the stream that it dipped
        from,
A riddled trammel-house bobbing its way
Toward a firm shore under the sea.

SKI SONG

At five my father made me skis,
My mother knit me cap and mitts
The carded fleece was spun out fine,
The straps were safe, a kick-free type,
At five when father made my skis.

With jack-knife skill my feet were winged,
With cunning stitch my head was cumbered.
On modest hills I soared and fell,
Flew down and herring-boned back up:
With jack-knife skill my feet were winged.

In time the childish thing put by,
The painted skis were handed on.
The cap was raveled and reknit.
The thongs were loosed—I chose my own
In time—the childish thing put by.

A woolen side one now wears in
On steeper slopes where bindings lock:
The laminated skis are new,
What turns the wind is still the same—
A woolen side one now wears in.

PATTERN PRETTY MUCH ESTABLISHED

Who keep to parks see it every season,
Rationalize or reason, so it goes in parks.

Near the further rushes, early clover-clean
And shy in spring, the cygnets mirroring

Start at breath in bushes, pick cake from bottle caps
By bench-lined June, tell August carmel corn

From tissue scraps, try close-cropped wings
Too soon, learn the limits of their lake too late.

Rationalize or reason, so it goes in parks—
And all the same, September swans are tame.

HIGH DESERT

> . . . and in the sixth place he imparted them
> understanding, and in the seventh speech, an
> interpreter of the cogitations thereof.
> —Ecclesiasticus

I.

Hard on a leveling off that gave us pause,
(The Sisters knelt, Three Fingered Jack fell back),
Early in a keen-cast dawn we drove
Out from the cattle town where we had slept.
We rolled along a field a farmer plowed,
A cleared strip where the ranchers set their planes;
Met an ancient windmill pumping wind
And a square of Herefords cropping at a hill.
Then, as house and rail and landmark sank,
We climbed on shimmering tides of smokeless blue,
Ascended breathless into terraced space
And cried the barrenness for name.

II.

Eye, what is the lay of the land?

Changing and changeless, vast and rimrock round.
The spotted fawn steps on the camel's grave;
The cougar mates in pinks, the rattler slides
Through arid sage and sleeps congealed on lava.
Picking his way among the heat-flaked bones,
The glossy ibis stalks a water hole
Now and again surveying the greasewood slopes,
The slick-running seas that break on basalt.
The land lies lost as a grain of light in the eye
That wakes and shuts the bitterroot cup.

Ear, what is the song and fury?

The rock dove's coo floats from a leafing branch,
Goes hollow down a creek's persistent rush.
The hurtling boulder slows, then mutes in sand,
Where the wild stallion's hooves have muffled out.
Jay screech, rat skitter and sweet redbird's note
Drown in the deep cronk of the stretched crane
Pulling uneasily on an evening gust.
Coyote snarls attend the fallen doe.
The sound is a dry gnat's buzz in the giant horn
That trumpets over the alkali flats.

What is the touch, the fingertip sketch?

The multitudinous crush of lava spawns
A pumice kiss, a fine obsidian edge.
Out of a tasseled carpet springs a clutch
Of buckbrush, the sting of beargrass,
The flick of a bug, the graze of soft fur.
Driving grit goes mud in a pelting shower
Then cracks that afternoon of the sun's heat.
The touch is velvet indifference, molten denial
And powder of blue moth wings in the hand
That cradles the scorched tablelands.

What of the scent, the perfumed response?

Sage and the pitchy tang of juniper boughs
Floating the stagnant marsh and the skunk's path;
Wild rose breath and yarrow pungence whirled
With carrion, with stench into full air;
A bluebottle waft of dung layered over
With willow fragrance blown from a river bank.
The dank of morning dew on the cheatgrass
Hovers the canyon, lodges a shaded wash.
The scent is a false peppercorn in the nostrils
That draw the aromas out of the fog.

What then is the taste and the savor?

Bitter and acrid, salt as the sea it was.
Berries are flat, the grapes dry in their skins.
The plum ripens small and the rose hips gnarl
But antelope browse on the tips of new sage.
The root of the rockrose yields a pure starch
And the foraging deer relish the sweetgrass.
First there is plenty. Late in the season the mouth
Consumes its own food and the hungerer.

III.
Where natural currents merge, the stream is roiled
And gift or curse, the boatman moves by oars.
Deluded for a time the course was set,
That simple placement asked of us no choice,
We fall the way we've come: the voice that drums
This landscape back as mirror or mirage,
That names this highest homeland, is our own.

FAREWELL AND HAIL

Such seasons I am told are always terminal.
Well then and good, for as certain Eskimos
Who abandon their aged to kindly tundras,
I have set a self, a more than time-gone crone,
On the keen-runnered sled for oblivion.
And even as those same Eskimos go about
The untroubled tracking of their land
Planing the permissive skies with oilsmooth looks
For a new coming of birds, so I await
The high clang of the first brant circling,
The green divulgence of a wrested clime.

Keith Hanson

SEASCAPE WITH BIRDS

for Bos

Between the fading seiner & the cliff
sun splinters on the silver
beach. Shipwreck or the swift descent
where now the gulls

crisscross to link name & landscape
rouses no raftered town.
Waves lifted from the amber kelp bed
crest with light. Across

a moment's stillness they advance
to the uniform rocks, caught
in ropes of foam. Six pewter birds
fragile as flowers unfold

at the sea's edge, their delicate
precise dance timed
to the green advance, the slow
retreat. Sea, locked

in a world of glass, breaks here
with birds, one face
from the looked for: by bright
silence to shout down

cold fathoms of fish. Whole years of sea
spill miracles to hide
their branching bones, the reaching
spar, the plucked skull.

TWO LOOK AT THE LAKE

Across the lake the masts of racing boats
descend, stretched thin through this apparent
metal to their solid grave. Along the shore
the willows are tall shivers in the wind
before the light falls, anchoring the sky.

Whatever frames the scene—Poussin, the cat
stretched on the sill—is all peripheral.
The poem lies somewhere between. And yet
somehow the scene is not the same for you,
the cat is not this cat, but brings a memory
of other summers, childhood, maiden aunts.

Behind the mirror of the lake, your boats
are motionless, remote, until the scene
is like a postcard. Even the willows change,
are somehow "more poetic," and the light
when it comes, to the wakening of birds,
comes with profounder thunder, not like it comes.

VOYAGE

The sea was wider than you dreamed at first
though not more deep. And what you found
was not what you had imagined. Well
you have gone there and have come back
no single shoreline accurate on the map
all of them (you might say) approximate
as if taken wholly from accounts of
drunken sailors, boasting in the bars.

What wonder travel folders warn against
the final integration, mystic or practical
(Eat nothing but thick rind fruits
while there). Imagined landscapes all
delude the eye with politics or prophecy.
Now you are home. Kept in a hinged
and secret room you mutter that you found
the beach littered with the bones of those
who tried to track the bloodstream to its
headwaters. Why bother trying to correct
the maps? They say you are mad, your
continents alive with remnant animals
the racketing of brilliant birds,
parades of solemn rabbits and
fantastic hats. Whatever you imagined
it was not that. Let them pretend
what they like. Now when you wake
you wake always in the same room, watching
mechanic spiders involve the corners.
There is nothing here to remind you
where you have been: from that lost
continent comes no remembrance whom they
harbor, brother or chance traveller.

ON A DEAD CAT IN MEXICO

Here lies what the quick body
has become—old bag of bones, mere
carpentry, a congress for all the flies
on Calle de Pepe Llano nearly.

Paws with their scimitars stretch
in a sunlight thick and unscrupulous
while fiestas of children follow me
chanting: Allo cinco, Allo money!

Toltec, Tarascan, Indian faces
with the eyes of raptorial birds,
and nowhere the sign of a personal loss
for the grey cat scrawny as cactus
gone like a minor civic virtue.

ENTRANCE INTO THE CITY

Dogs at the gates of day
with vigorous alarm forecast
all strangers. From towers
on the hour the tall clocks
ring to please themselves—
clang clang, a flattering gift
for the brazen doves.

Elsewhere in the listing city
crowds rich as timothy
grow on streetcorners, stand
motionless, bend to the rumors,
expect from a cloudless sky
the pronouncement of carnivals.
Maps in a number of colors
report the selection of streets
they are likely to come by.

For days in the dark museums
curious schoolchildren
flourishing voices like pincers
have filed past the kings in cases,
learning to recognize and name
masters of vast desert kingdoms
still stretching somewhere
under a lemon sun.

When finally they appear—
the chiming acrobats, lions
with violent manes, the captives
chained or in cages, and the long
columns of soldiers (some selling
their colored maps and looking
quite life-like) —the children
who have all been taught three ways
to tell the true from the false dead
explode with flowers, "hurrah! hurrah!"
and the crowds set like clocks
to expect kings with curly beards
only pretend to be disappointed.

Later, in the comfortable suburbs
old men weep on picket fences,
crying "Time! O cruel season!"
This too they pretend
not to enjoy. And in the park
where the dogs of summer
drowse in pavilions of parasols
the colorful children are already
translating into dull history
their lost, holy wars.

STATISTIC

This is the scene exactly as it was,
the ruined flies on the windowledge,
damp coffee grounds, a knife, a rose
from the wall, clogging the sink.
Two bulbs burned in the sockets of brass claws.
This is the scene exactly as it was.

The papers tell how she hated her mother,
arranged the kill, hid, sat in the cold flat,
hearing the harbor whistles. There
with her lover the abstract Kid
she watched the rose on the wall repeat,
a day and a day. He didn't return,
Persephone tearing the fairytale to shreds
like a handkerchief. There's nothing more.

She set her wild blood free on its course,
she stopped it cold in its tracks.
When the bills ran up, she cut her closest ties.
Time, for a little time after she died,
chirped like a cricket tied to her wrist.

SIDESHOW

Under the weight of souvenirs,
the paper lei, the monkey on a stick
we hear the summer gathered in a spiel.
Such wonders crowd our common place!
Such grim perfection of astounding skill!
We envy the deft magicians who produce
soiled handkerchiefs from the pure air,
wince at the crabbed proportions of a dwarf,
doubt stubbornly the dog-faced boy.
This is the mummy, imperfect now,
a hole where his sawdust innards spill.
No sign of viscera. We stare unmoved.

Like Simon simple to the fair we pass
the last cash barrier to seek our fortune
in the cards, discount the future

witnessed by our hand (a change of scene,
new friends, perhaps a violent end),
peer at the wrenching mirrors where
we're patched parsed withered and askew,
our vast head dandled on a stalk
so sprung our very name hangs loose.

How shall we greet these prodigies
who share no Africa, observe no past?
who wear no saving motto blazed
above the ineradicable heart?
Disjoined, hand arm & eye at odds,
we stand exhibited before these cold
observers like an awkward guest.
When shall our crooked kingdom come,
our cracked & elementary bones construct
their sole authentic skeleton?

Blind lights annoy the vacant air
where possibilities by life grown large
prevent the gaudy miracle to join
this audience, to read our fortune
quartered in the knavish mirrors, back
into the patient deck. We wait.
Behind the tent a cricket chirrs.
Torn posters scatter on the walk.
The moon has vanished like a palmer's coin.
We stiffen, hesitate, turn back.
Beyond the park, the gypsies & the clowns
are changing in the silent dark.

OLD MAN

April to October
under the only tree
he spoke nonsense about
miscegenation and the gods,
filled with his learning as
spiders are full of their own webs.

"My fields are lunatic with trees!"
he cried. "Their black limbs
blossom but do not bear—
nothing I pray for prospers—
and even this frail blossoming
has to be braced against wind."

O he was that prince at random,
Spain or China, what does it matter:
nobility of mind
is everywhere the same.

Suspicious, haughty,
October to April
he read dead ladies
to their drafty tombs.

"Kind birds are these," he sang,
"who spend time's song
against the windowpane.
Hear them! I take good news
from anywhere far. Next month
they'll move me outside."

Fond prince, you sleep their springtime through.
What eye can fool the patient wind,
refuse the brilliant sand, or spoil
the vigor of the sea?
What god, what hero born in Troy
wastes on the edge of Town?